Daughter of the Thames

Daughter of the Thames

Poems

Fathieh Saudi

Lotus Foundation

First published in the UK by The Lotus Foundation

www.lotusfoundation.org.uk

Cover : Loneliness by Claudia Coppola

ISBN 978-0-9559951-7-0

Printed and bound in Great Britain by Bell & Bain Ltd., Glasgow

Contents

9

The water - its heart is pure.
It has become my teacher.
Po Lo-t'ien, Chinese poet

Preface

Though I have been passionate about poetry since adolescence, I never dared to write poems until I reached my early fifties. I thought it was a man's privilege. Maybe my poems were sleeping in my unconscious mind for a long time before finding their way into life.

Coming to live in London and after going through a difficult period in my life, I felt I was teetering on the edge of everything - even of life itself. I felt traumatized, uprooted, unprotected, and exiled from the self, severed from my identity and my own language. I wondered then, what is language, what are words, visions, images and thoughts? Are they a way of communicating between the self and others? What about communicating with the self, finding the language of the self? I decided then to write in English. It was as though the language had adopted me. Writing in a new language was liberating, as it allowed me to overcome many conscious and unconscious barriers and taboos, and to discover the space for my own creativity. My poems became my only voice - me the speechless, the silenced. And I decided to rebirth myself through poetry.

My poems move between the personal and the collective, between the private and the public, maybe like my life from my early years, when I was deeply aware of a sense of injustice in the world, but at the same time a sense of its beauty, and also of a desire to be free, and I carried this all along my joyful, painful journey.

I wrote most of my poems by the Thames. Close to the river I felt relaxed, at peace, at home, connected with my deep self. It was as though I were holding a mirror through which I could see my past, my experiences, my pain, my struggles and fragilities, while continuing a complex dialogue, owning a voice and giving meaning to my existence and soul, certainly guided by an instinct for survival, beauty and hope. Unexpectedly the Thames offered me protection and the feeling that there was still some magic in life. I became daily more attached to the river. It was like a growing love. I decided to rebirth my life there. I always think life and poetry are pockets full of miracles.

Fathieh Saudi

I

Birth of a language

Metaphors

The footpath, as I step
forward, feels tender. I am
smoke billowing toward
wide open space.
                    When
my shoulders give way, I borrow
the wings of an eagle.
                    When
my crutches abandon me, I walk
like a ballet dancer.
However
insightful I try to be,
I can't write a perfect poem:
life rushes towards me

before becoming words.

Searching for a language

I had longed to find a language
for my feelings, speak of life
like the dance of a stream,
take wing.

The stranger said: all languages
belong to me, keep away from them,
live your feelings

in silence. I became speechless,
my paralyzed emotions
hurt me.

The stranger said: words
are my kingdom and you
are my slave.

Now the page I am writing on
glides away. Even paper
can rebel.

Kneading

Once upon a time, my Aleph went astray,
my life shrank, my womb was sucked dry.

Sitting by the Thames, I recall
the hands of my mother kneading bread,
mixing drops of water with the paste,
turning the flour into dough.

Beside the Thames, I knead
my shattered letters anew:
one, seven, ten, twenty-six,
more.

My water-born language.

Aleph is the letter A in Arabic.

Convoy

Words in opposing motion
journey like lightning,
fall tenderly onto the earth,
become equatorial rain.

Words adrift in an ocean, touching
each other, reaching out,
heading for a wave breaker,
sometimes rescue one another,
sometimes heartbroken.

Words emerge from my gentlest dream,
awakening unconscious words
from a century of sleep.
There are many fluid roads to tenderness.

Don't know

I look in the mirror. Mine is a pale reflection.
Who is there? Is anyone there?

My steps drag me to the wilderness.
I listen to the vibrations of the earth,

rest under the shade of a fig tree,
drift over the river, connect
with the wisdom of rippling water.

In my mirror, I was there. The child, the teenager,
the sadness, the happiness, and a rainbow
came into view. Suddenly I-don't-know

turns into I-know. From the mirror
I-know begins to emerge.

Imaginary crossing

I don't pretend my life
is a perfect circle. Reality
strokes my fragile shoulders.

Green grass grows under my feet,
I have a new name, live in an unknown city,
adopt another language, give birth to a new self.

Can I make my nightmares lucid, escape
the reflections of the past? it's time
to cross the viaduct back to life.

Kew Bridge

I stumble across a labyrinthine street.
The earth moves faster than my steps.
How can I reach my home,
my only sanctuary.

Seaweed caresses my thighs,
mud dampens my feet,
my wings are violet,
my dress is white.

My language falls
like autumn leaves,
with no rustling of a word to rescue me.
Like a wounded gull my soul whirls.

I am the bride of the river,
I have one face, only one. A face
transparent as pure water.

Looking for me

My homeland was far away,
my father dead,
my mother left behind,
my loved ones had gone away.

I stopped receiving letters.
My inbox was empty.
My phone fell silent.

My body was suddenly ageing.
My mind, emptied of memories,
slammed the door of thought.
The *khasmin* alone whispered at my window.

From faraway an alphabet came
shattering the silence into a necklace
of words. A winged word

was looking for me, I caught sight of it
flying just above my head.

Illusions

What illusion should I adopt
to keep alive? Lightening

on a dark summer night, brightening
the earth for a millionth of a second,

drops of water in a stream
dreaming of becoming a river,

candlelight in a cave
yearning to be the sun,

a butterfly, when it glimpses a caterpillar's
wings, turning into a falcon,

the echo of a foreign language
becoming familiar.

Birth of a poem

Once the vagabond asked what attracted me
to him: the person, the poetry, or the poet?
I opened my eyes wide, no words came.

Between sips of wine, and laughing-
his lips were thin, eyes like slits-
he went on asking his question. For

a long time I forgot it. The vagabond
passed away, but still the question. What?
My conscious attraction was to the poet,

my unconscious to poetry,
my childlike to the person.
How could I tell them apart?

Could I save anything, my body, my soul,
my being, even my sense of poetry?

My heart !How can we save the poetry
of life? A few seconds are left,
only a few. My heart! Beat faster,

release me from the tunnel, show me
the way, don't abandon me
to permanent eclipse.

My heart, exhausted, whispers to my being:
"Give your thoughts freedom, dance
with words, breathe with alphabets,
reach out, surrender to the ocean
even if you can't swim." " Trust me,"

trust me, my heart whispers.
"Write down one line, one line only,
you can save your poetry of life.

Let your pencil be the boat,
your feelings the safety rope,
your words the water,

then all will flow softly,
a line of a poem will be born."

II

Daughter of the Thames

John the Baptist

To wash my body,
wherever I am, a few
litres of water is all I need.

To purify the past in my body,
to heal the wounds it holds,
how many oceans?

I step back to my childhood,
to the River Jordan, enter.
The water is crystal, serene the current.

John the Baptist cleansing the world
with pearls of water.

The stars shimmer, create
a home for me. An infinite
sun revives my body.

Shades of tears

A few clouds, a blue sky
and shades of grey.

Will it rain?
What colour will the rain be?

A necklace of tears in my heart,
white, blue, or grey. A few
drops in the clouds, many
in my soul, thousands

behind my eyes. One
beneath my lids.

Daughter of the Thames

A luminescent shadow, one day
at nightfall, arose from the river.

Dark waters, muddy waters, troubled,
where I dreaded the end. The river has

halted its flow, silent
for a second, sparkling for another.

Light from the depths,
erupts through the invisible.

Stillness offers me a final choice,
the river a safety net.

Its laughing water sends me warmth,
connects me to my very soul.

I become, in that moment,
the daughter of the Thames.

Wounded soul

Pain transfixing the soul, the body
explodes into invisible atoms.

Blood evaporates. Dagon breathes
air into my lungs. Bacchus

restores my strength. Spring tides reset
the beating of my heart.

Imaginary city

I follow my steps to unknowable destinations,
stagger along the path of darkness,
travel to the outer edges of the city,

touch the margins of my life.
At sunset in Somerset
unforeseen bridges emerge,

leading me to knowable places.
My room is next to the river,
my window open to a passing train.

I see a city floating in my heart.

Flight of exhausted birds

The first hummingbird hit the bridge,
fell.

The river, saddened by shattered wings,
wept.

Its water rose above the parapet.
The flock passed over.

Home with no roof

My steps don't trouble the rocks.
The earth seems solid.

The surface of the river looks so tranquil,
deep as mother earth.

Four wooden posts have been abandoned
to the current where Buddha forgot to build a roof
for his floating home.

Womb

1

Can I
live between these two?

Womb of my mother: warmth,
heartbeats, whispers surrounding me.

Womb of the Thames: floating,
lightness, pulses of a faraway ocean.

2

I grew up between whispering dunes,
sand in my eyes, on my lips.
The only taste I knew was thirst.

By the Thames,
I expand in the space of a welcoming womb.
It's time to create my life again.

The eighth day

I lost my father, all my daddies.
Orphaned, though childhood is far away,

who is stretching time?
The Thames promises to give me re-birth,

I dive into her waters,
emerge with dry skin, air fills my lungs.

Born on the eighth day of the week,
I am free from all my fathers!

Avalanche

Thoughts hammer at the walls of my courage.
An avalanche of thoughts comes out of the darkness.

The ocean tunes my thoughts.
The river embraces their tumbling chaos.

The speed of my thoughts harmonises with the cosmos.
The avalanche is over.

River language

Lips of water kissing,
fish dance in liberty.
A river is born.

Water dressed in red
"This is my blood,"
the prophet said.

Water of a river
Thames Ganges Nile
flowing each moment towards their destiny.

I can walk to the current of the river,
hieroglyph are my alphabet,
my language a bridge to life.

The ocean is my home.

III

Places in time

Continents

I learned the realms of the four seasons,
the geography of five continents.

Today I discover
the world has six continents,

the greatest the one inside,
the landscape of the Self

where continents touch.
I am wondering how to get there.

I learn to travel through
to land.

Beirut

My childhood taught me the alphabet.
Beirut taught me the language of life

and for her I raise an altar in my heart.

How does a city come to be in pain,
like you and I?

Beirut, city of the soul, my body embraces you.
What am I, an observer or even a witness?

Can I stop consciousness knocking at my heart?
What can we do to stem the flood?

In Beirut I saw the walls of the world
built with bombs, with molten iron.

In Beirut I understood the meaning of life.
I touched the essence of humanity.

Beirut, o remain with me
protect the rhythm of my soul,

for the sake of hope,
of a just world without walls.

Crossroads

The nightingale lies at a crossroads,
her heart shriveled, her wings
collapsed. At dawn life left her.

Maybe, a stranger passing
will place her under her favourite tree.
She was fortunate to live and die at a crossroads.

Jaffa

Jaffa, spouse of the sea, a home
for the last lost sailor.

Listen to the waves, smell the breeze,
open your heart, and Jaffa will embrace you.

His tender voice drew me to him,
sitting on his wooden bench, facing the sea.

Strangely his eyes didn't blink,
was he totally blind?

magic images pursued me. I returned
to his bench. Nothing but
echoes of his visions with me now,

I felt Jaffa embracing me.

Jaikour

On my twentieth birthday, I dreamt
my daughter's name would be Jaikour.

I imagined her beautiful, graceful,
a smile that outshone a comet,
a heart that melted pearl.
She would always be generous.

Jaikour, Jaikour.
I never ventured there,
a small village next to the Euphrates,
birthplace of Alsayab, my favourite
poet a long time ago.

In his dreams,
from his hospital bed in London,
between cries of pain, he called
incessantly "Jaikour, Jaikour."

I gave Jaikour a soul. Today,
thirty years later, though my child
is not yet born, though Jaikour
was erased by wars,

I continue to love
the mystery of the word.
Jaikour, Jaikour.

Jaikour is the birth place of the Iraqi poet Bader Shaker Alsayab. In his poetry, Jaikour is a symbol of fertility and salvation.

A room with no oxygen

1

A nightmare besieges me in every corner,
my vocal chords fall silent.
I lose consciousness,
become the echo
of a receding life.

2

Here life begins and comes to an end.
A window overlooking a cemetery,
a door opening onto an enclosure.
The window is veiled with lace,
the door surrounded by barbed wire.
What space remains for me?

3

A room in a suburb,
yellow sofas, books I loved,
carpet in rainbow colours,
music melancholic like my steps,

walls layered with multiple deaths,
windows and landscapes,
door with no key.

4
There will be no incantation
no orchestra, no halleluiah,
it's time for the exile of the self.

Songs for a terrace

1

On the terrace you weep.
Tears quench the thirst of oleander,
yet a cascade of tears
may drown the pine trees.

2

On the terrace tears flow.
Will they rouse these plants?
Maybe they can expand,
giving you roots again.

3

On the terrace you are eager to escape
from despair and death.
Would you learn the wisdom
of the seeds resisting cold and drought
to become the trees of the future?

4

We live on the terrace, he
and I. We adore
its dimensions,
its orbits, but
we live there each alone.

5

He lives on the terrace
happy with his plants
and tales coming to life.
You lives on the terrace
seeking to grasp the grains of life,
to surrender to the soul of roots.

6

He lives on the terrace in winter.
In summer I care for plants resisting despair.
Is that why I planted them
in the chill of winter?

7

You put on the light every evening
though you are the only one to return.
Each night your heart beats with joy.
Maybe the unthinkable will surprise you.

8

On the terrace,

grass, seashells,

cockles filled with of silence.

Is this why suddenly you feel nostalgic

for a visitor who will never return?

IV

Expressions

My first neighbour in London

"live while you may and live in clover,

tomorrow you will be dead all over."

Ogden Nash

Helen offers me a bed, the first in my naked home,
a camp-bed I will care for all my life.

Behind my window she murmurs:
I have lived my life, I don't regret a thing.
She recites her beloved Ogden Nash.

Helen questions me often.
What did I have for breakfast?
How many letters did I get last week?

Helen, I do care about you.
In the silence of ageing,
we share an unspoken tenderness.

Helen sometimes has deeper questions.
Did you like Pavarotti on Sundays?
Do you enjoy your solitude?

Helen lives in the shadows of her life. Each day
she opens her book of memories.
It is her birthday today.

Helen and I continue to wait for
a pocketful of miracles.

A thousand and one times

I wasn't Sheherazade.
There was no king to listen to my stories,
no prince to grant me one more day of life.
I was telling stories to my self. I even
invented poems.

I travelled to my childhood,
wrote stories, some finished,
others as yet half imagined.
Recalling them in silence
kept me alive.

Oh, now I am Sheherazade
and the king.

I have to listen to the landscapes
of myself, to stay alive
time and time again,
a thousand and one times.

Mona Lisa

Good morning Mona Lisa,
my walls mirror your mysterious smile.

Good evening Mona Lisa
my heart is pounding.

Concert

To Mikis Theodorakis

The soul's whispers resonate,
the seeds awaken, the body
becomes a bird. Rhythms

intensify, unite with the whole,
give a soul to the human voice,
transcend the earth's pain.

We climb the steps of the Acropolis,
walk in the lanes of Jerusalem.

The heart grows bigger,
the light of hope brightens,
we feel a sense of collective gratitude,

the creative majesty of a human soul.

I long for this connection

A young seal lying on the shore,
his face seems strangely human;
anxious pupils,
turbulent feelings,
full of tenderness,

fearing the nearby human beings.
Rubbing his eyes,
wondering where to turn,

should he trust human beings,
wait for a faraway mother,
flee into the open ocean?

He and I, aquatic beings once.
I dream of surviving in the deep,
of breathing, together, above and under water?

Vertical

To Sylvia Plath

Desperate, I ask the blind to show me
the way. I long to save my life.

She wasn't my mother
yet she gave me life again.

I contemplate her face,
glimpse her tears, sense her anger.

I reach the space around her,
grasp the stars of life.

She teaches me
to step towards my river,

walk on water like a seagull,
leap onto a transparent line of life,

build a home from the alphabet,
fly with wet wings.

She teaches me to cross a bridge
at the edge of life,

survive a storm,
stay vertical.

V

Journey through the dark

Exhausting the memory

To Ursula James

The sea's wild wind storms across the sand.
With each breath of that wild wind,
his face takes on a different shape
between nothingness and wholeness.

I sit for hours at the train window.
Trees speed past, allow me to go forward.
Once again I return to the seashore.
My body can't turn into a breaker. I open
my lungs to the air, to the waves,
walk ahead.

My steps guide me into familiar alleyways.
I wandered here once before. In the noisy pub
could I shape his face from ten others?
I am not an artist able to sculpt faces.
I am not a musician able to invent
the sound of a voice.
I am what I know.

Here, memories invade me violently,
tenderly, fearfully.
He is not here any more,
to frighten me. My heart
beats like an eagle in a cage.
Memories are becoming my prison.
I am what I know.

I want to tire out my memories:
his shadow sitting facing me;
the white hair, the hidden smile,
the small dark eyes, anger in his features
sculpted in stone.

My teacher said, "Relive the past, dive deep,
let it bombard you, drown you,
let it flood you, then you can dive out."

My memories flood me like a drowning
bird in an unknown ocean.
I come out breathless.

Land of forgotten things

My nightmare expanded into a yearmare.

Who am I? What is memory?
I have forgotten.

My past was wiped out in a second.
Like cities after an earthquake,
the rooms of my memory fell apart.
Just fragments.

I forgot I was a doctor, a successful
Woman; my awards, my struggles.
I forgot I had a family.
I forgot those magical days.

I rotated around my axis, no compass to guide me.
I was only a shapeless body with wounded memories.
Had have I been so since my birth?
What more was left to forget?

Shattering

A child is only learning the shapes of unfamiliar objects,
when he breaks a toy every day for fun.

A man breaks the dignity of his lover many times,
enjoys looking at her shattered soul.

It didn't occur to him
a woman isn't a child's toy.

Wolf Man

He has mastered the map of the world's caves.
Each day he prowls around in his grotto,
waiting for a new victim. Teeth

in his heart, in his mind. He swallows
 his children one by one. His mouth
bulging with flesh.

This wolf has no one face,
he can metamorphose into endless wolves.
Victims can never evade him.

He masks his anger,
his shadow. He has no
eyes, only rage.

The wolf as predator.
Ever he was.

In the dark

I know you desire me dead.
Yet I am still alive!

Then will you say:
"she was a kind woman, she was
my only friend, she left behind
a void in my life?"

You are more fluent talking to the dead.
Would you, then, in your endless nightmares,
talk to me?

My being alive irritates your conscience:
no one must discover your hidden faces,
your alter egos.

Which is less costly for you; me dead
or your restless conscience?

From this second I am alive, whatever
you may wish, plan,
or dream about.

I will free myself from your destructiveness,
from all your nightmare prisons.

It will be a long journey
yet I will get there.

Augustus

He drifts from city to city,
always leaving luggage at the station.

His anger follows him everywhere.
Nothing can contain it.

Like terrifying shadows at midnight,
violent darkness from childhood torments him.

Every city becomes a prison, smaller or bigger.
The vast prison inside him, he never perceives.

He imagines himself the emperor Augustus.
Who would dare to disobey him?

Ovid was exiled to Tomis, a town whose language
he had never even whispered before;

others to caves, or out of life,
in ships sailing to a dark world.

He exiles those closest to him,
every one he touches must suffer and suffer
without end.

Kingdom of fear

She was a full citizen
in his kingdom of fear:
had only the right to
whatever style he invented.

Its foundations set deep
into the earth, Her walls
were built of terror; a petrifying
black web of roof covered her.
She lived in a permanent eclipse: the moon
dimmed, frost silenced the oceans.

Woman's refuge

Pink walls,
chequered floor,
white ceiling,

an alarm in the middle
with flashing light. Will fire
flare up here or within me?

A sink in one corner,
a window open to the seasons.

The walls change from rose to grey,
the narrow bed embraces my body
preventing me from falling.

The bed cover comes from Samarqand
red velvet embroidered with silver and gold.

My room is my queendom.

Folding my home

Knowing how to turn the pages of a book,
today I am learning how to fold up my home.

I fold the curtains, the carpets,
the masks, the photographs hanging on the walls.

I fold the unfoldable
uprooted pillars of my memories.

I never imagined I would be able to layer my memories
like the pages of a sacred book.
One by one.

Silent explosion

The earth knows earthquakes
mothers apprehend labour pains
oceans discern the mood of the moon.

She lived a physical rape,
today she is witnessing the rape of her life.
How many tsunamis in one life?

Hidden

It was a long time ago
but the pain is still needle-sharp.

Remember how you conjured
illusions to veil that past,

embraced the suffering of the world,
created metaphors to give the beast beauty.

You tried over and over again
but it continues to hurt.

That clotted blood on your white coat,
you can't scrape away even to this day.

A few seconds of one person's life,
anguish hidden throughout the life of another.

Marriage

The first day:
she feels weightless
swans offer her their wings
she could fly forever.

Dressed in a purple blouse, yellow trousers,
her teenage bicycle races with the wind.
She navigates the city,
her hair caresses the breeze
her smile is so wide
freedom radiates around her.

Her town seems more beautiful than ever before
the sun shines at midnight,
her empty room is a palace,
her wings reach every shore.
She is in love with the whole universe.

The last day:
in vain she searches for her name

her left shoulder is dislocated
her home a dark corner
her vision blurred
her hair turned white
her mind shaking, her heart
has relinquished the light of life.

Haha!

You can bite anything: my shoulder, my thigh.
You believed you could conquer far-off dictators.

I share no history with them.
I share some history with you,
them and you, me and you.
I became the victim.

Can you evict the dictators dwelling inside you?
Your final way out is to keep them alive.

To live is to accept all the winds,
not wounds,

winds, not wounds.
For the winds I have windbreaks,
for wounds I have no more blood.
Enough bleeding in my life.

Tsunami waves

Water has memory, I believe.
The ethereal body has another memory
vast inside us.

Voracious waves, human anguish,
I sense each of them.
I lived them too.

How could I tread over
a shattered mudscape?
How did I survive?

The devastation, the uprooting
by a human being you thought close to you.
Whom would you believe in now?

I merged with all those images:
my heart was thrown out,
lying breathless across a rock,
my lungs hanging on a palm tree,

my broken arms landing in front of a luxury hotel,
shadows of my legs walking in an unknown town.

There will be no Ark, no Noah to save me.
My tsunami.

Edges

I glimpse many edges: of a bed, a river, a vision.
I encounter others: of despair, loneliness, drowning.

I foresee other edges: of madness, unfaith, deception,
of losing a last strand that could have bound up
the ravaged world,

the fluidity of edges volatile enough
to make me smile at each of them.

The *Khamsin* reshapes a sandy mountain, enough
to keep me waiting for the breath of life to come.

Childhood traumas

She often wondered about his childhood.
He never asked about hers.

After twenty years, the question was still
vivid in her mind.

Though she overcame what ravaged her childhood,
she would never know what happened in his.

They would never become equals. She
was always protective of others
and herself.

He was always destructive of others.
Never of himself.

Resonances

Ice touching her face in midsummer,
shadows of roses bleeding on her wall,
animal skin lying on the floor.

How could she say her lover was like Cain?

Facing the shadows

Her grandfather ended the life of a man,
ran away to India,
was never punished.

One day her son passed away.
She had never spoken tenderly to him.

She wandered painfully all her life,
became a priest, a lawyer, a rebel,
yet she never freed herself.

How to become free of a life's violence denied?

The fall

Often in my childhood I fell
from a roof or a sycamore tree
or down the ten steps that lead to the Roman Nymphium.

I witnessed other falls:
my father into pain,
my friend into despair.

I read of more:
Kilimanjaro cascading into the rainforest,
the Nile descending from the Equator.

How to protect consciousness from falling?
Jesus on the cross.
No more falls.

Belated discovery

Let me live!
I whisper day and night.
Stop calling me into your greyness.

Didn't you drag me into your caves,
didn't you darken our home at midday?

Didn't I care for you like a lover, a poem,
protect you from imaginary bullets,
from nails on the wall?

Didn't I hold back so you could lighten your life,
so the mysteries of your grey world could brighten.

Didn't I melt into all the shapes you intended,
become the sponge for your soul's torments?

I did. Maybe innocently, maybe not,
hope was a candle in my heart,
healing love a dream.

Some grey zones are impenetrable
even under the rays of the equatorial sun.

Violence

A few letters. Oonnff.
No more. In her mother tongue
it sounds like a breath.

A slave on a pirate ship,
waves in the soul;

a Somali refugee on a boat,
dreaming of reaching a welcoming land;

a teenager running away from despair,
a rapist awaiting her at crossroads;

a rebel dreaming of a free world,
only leaving the dictator's prison after his last breath;

an aborigine warming his body with a blanket,
unaware of the deadly disease it holds;

a woman in love, between one dream and another,
killed by her brother, "to cleanse his honour", he said,

Does she strive to protect herself or
the first human being who suffered?
She can't heal her own pain, so could she
pretend to heal others? Cruelty

is a chain forged by violence.
Starting at any point, intertwined labyrinths
of agony may go off at a tangent, any tangent,
whether the tenth or the thousandth way of violence.

Meeting with the king

Tonight, tonight
will it be my last night?

I will be in the arms of the angry king.
He will crush my lungs. An unspoken word
will be my last breath.

Which word will it be,
which word will end my life,
in what language?

Will it be a piercing scream or silent?
Will it be painful?

My steps dragged me to his palace
a westerly wind blew on my face
the palm trees ached with cold.

I saw my death clamouring in his eyes:
he had already killed me
yet I was still alive!

Suddenly a rebel grew inside me:
deadened feelings can't decide my end,
I would choose my own death.

The king said: what last wish do you utter?
I murmured: a glass of water.

The drops of water turned into a lake
the lake into a river
the river into a sea,
I was in a womb again.

With my last sip of water
a pristine voice formed within me
words opening into many shapes.

I had never heard my voice before
my words were tender, telling
stories from unfamiliar lands:

babies born from a rainbow
wounds healed by a smile
the moon dropping rain
the sun warming midnight,

humans born from water
flying mountains embracing the clouds
grass growing tall to shelter lovers
hearts speaking through time and space.

How many months, years
had passed away? The king's eyes
kept open. A white feather
has touched his heart.

Tonight I know, the king can't break my life
tonight is the last of the thousand and one nights
tonight I will leave his palace
tonight my life is mine.

Abou Ghraib never existed

These two words hurt.
Every image is painful.
All are blurred. To transform
them into words took her seven years.

Scenes pass before her eyes,
disturb her thoughts,
paralyze her imagination.
Words take shape out of agony.

The blurred images are clearer,
like shadows drawing closer
through the dark, made
more visible, completely visible.

Wars blitz the mind before the shelling of bombs.
Why do wars start on earth,
who ignites the first spark?

The lights of the Albert Bridge, her guardian.
Trust the light.

Abou Ghraib began within the walls of her home.
Human beings may disintegrate ahead of war
as if to foretell an imminent apocalypse.
She witnessed his disintegration,
His facial expressions became like the dictator s,
the same hazy eyes, the icy cold.

She saw Brigadier Lynndie England,
invading every space. All citizens are subject to occupation
by harassment, intimidation, humiliation, or worse.

The time of torture began.
"It's time for you to die,
there is no role for you in my life,
you don't exist anymore he said.
His humanity plummeted into a lethargic coma.

The lights of the Albert Bridge shine across the page.
She needs to see clearly through the darkness.

It took her years even to stutter a word again,
longer to learn to speak.

Dictator, warlords, occupiers pretend innocence.
Nothing had happened anywhere
from Roman times to the present day.
There had been no crime, no massacre,
not even one death.

How could she grasp the netter world?
the destructiveness?
How resist annihilation?

Images caught in a web:
dogs biting naked prisoners
men chained like animals
dried blood on the floor
men hooded with plastic bags
shackled in rusty chains
hungry dogs frightening them
bodies heaped on one another
human beings raped to the soul.

Hajj Ali standing balanced on a cardboard box.
Gus with a dog collar around his neck,
Brigadier Lynndie dragging him.
Agonized men bathing in excrement
naked men piled up like a rubbish tip.

Abuse planned in dark caves.
Brigadier Lynndie is there,
she is here.

Many other Abou Ghraibs took place
in villages, cities, caves, homes,
between enemies, tribes, families, neighbours.

Traumatic memories know no time
they can perish in seconds
or last a lifetime.

She struggled to defend her dignity,
her right to live. Who would stand
by her?

She lived in fear those seven years,
travelled into deepest silence,
disabled to the bone.

Tonight she will let go of her fear.
The sunset falls on the trees, lights brighten the river's face
and the winter leaves wait for the promised light of dawn.

Albert Bridge is shining
she will find her way back home,
clearer than ever before.

VI

Eclipse of the body

Childhood

She was only a child. Her feet
hadn't yet touched the earth.

As she lay in her bed
her world became a vault of terror,
she couldn't move her limbs,
her whole body. Her heart

beat like chaotic drums, her screams
aborted in her chest, her bed
wet with her tears. Or her fear.
She couldn't tell which.

Ali the local sheikh was reciting
incomprehensible words, slapping her cheeks
to expel the demons. She couldn't grasp
what was happening

fever, paralysis, demons, possession.
She was only a year old.

She felt even more paralysed,
as if mountains crushed her body.

Fathi her brother, moved by her tears,
threw out Mr Ali, carried her
to a hospital. It was only a virus.
She might survive, she might not.

It took her fifty five years
to grasp the tragedy of that first loss,
the dormant insecurity which had always
dwelt with her.

No more Mr. Alis.
Never again.

Deaths

Death is always sudden, tragic,
even when it takes a hundred years.

Some deaths are graceful as a ballet dancer,
others fearful like a Medusa's face;

some deaths we walk towards consciously,
some unconsciously as in a dream;

some we are rushed towards at the speed of light,
at other times we crawl tortoise-like towards them;

some deaths we dress in rainbow colours,
others frighten and torture us.

Perhaps you may die
and no one will hear about it.

Or maybe you will pass away
with tenderness surrounding you.

Once in a while we die
in the silence of the self.

Some deaths we live before their time.
There is never a good time for death to come.

Wounds with no scars

Sutures, fresh or old.
Wounds of all ages,
waiting to heal.

Each wound carries the memory of another,
sutures shaping themselves into lines,
searching out a way to attain invisibility.

Parts of us wanting to communicate
yet all in agony. One strives to walk,
another to escape.

It's a life journey for the parts of the body,
for the whole body, even.

Body and mind

I wondered how to halt the emotional holocaust,
"if there is no body, there can be no more pain!"

These growing calcifications in my left breast, in my lung,
dangerous chaotic cells so close to my heart.
My body's ultimate final appeal.

Am I the wounded healer?
How can I re-imagine my very existence?

One hundred fingers

Her wings were full of dust. She plummeted
into mother earth.

She held her breath,
scrabbled deep in the rocks
so much to remove, to push away,

digging with her ten fingers,
with her hundred fingers.
Her heart shrank.

The earth's womb was filled with fire and rock.
No water to quench the blaze.

Her last breath, an eruption of strength,
a tiny space opened between layers of rock,
she forced the tip of one finger through,

found a space to pass, then another and another,
until from the darkness her hand emerged.

Her body felt a fresh
breath coming from a shy sun.

A butterfly moved inside.
Another flutter of her wings,
and rocks around crumbled.

She was resurrected
on the earth.

Distant wishes

Tonight I long to navigate the Thames,
dream of days yet to come:
see another full moon
close my eyes without fear
learn about forgiveness
hold hope under my eyelids
build an altar for love in my heart.

To forestall another unexpected death,
and trust the cadence of the cosmos
for many thousands days.

Faces for death

Be a singer, be
Venus the tender,

be a kiss on my wounds,
not a sword on my flesh,

be comforting as a womb,
not merciless as a barbarian,

be my beloved tonight,
but remain faithful to life,

don't become me,
just let me be myself,

come to me a rainbow in a dream,
don't become too real,

let me lie on the wet grass,
hear the earth's words,

be my beginning,
not my end,

be my enlightenment,
not the darkness.

Timelessness

He shaved the remains of my hair, laughed,
said my bald head looked nice, as
perfectly spherical as mother earth.

He selected a honey-coloured wig
for me. My wig, which suits my head
perfectly, is called Timeless.

In my cancer I am freed. How
can I perfectly measure the passing
of the hours?

Living in a timeless world
the layers of fear dissipate
the burden of the future dissolves.

O I adore my fresh bald head.

VII

Compass of hope

Earth

The scene is so besieged,
there is no room for colour.

Blue desires to talk with green,
red yearns for black,
and white feels sorry for grey.

Blue soars high into the seventh sky,
the sea in love becomes its mirror;
feeling shy, green turns into a shade of blue;
red in turmoil revolts, becoming blood,
grey withdraws in despair. Yellow,

alone at a turning-point
decides to shine. And the space around me
fills with every colour.

Only a miracle can set me free,
the power of my mind:
nourishing as the first drop of breast milk,

meticulous as a creator placing the moon,
tender as a womb, passionate
as a first lover's kiss, vigilant
as an astronaut leaving earth, vast
as the memories of generations longing for
cosmic knowledge. Millions of cells
faithful to every second of my existence.

And yet again the fragility of my mind:
compelled by one haunting thought,
revisiting flashbacks,
decoding thousands of messages from my heart,
tumbling into hidden labyrinths,
torn between being slave and saviour,
a mind dreaming of turning the world.
Longing to protect me in each moment

Exactly three years ago today
I was in a plane. Did I invent my trip today?
The nightmares, unwanted, are here again,

but today I am the director.
I know each second of the film
before I shoot it.

So just be.
It's delightful to be.

At dawn, scorched
by the remains of last night's fire,
the walls of time suddenly seem soft.
The soul in waves.

I sit next to my self,
Longing, within the rooms
of my heart, to reach a decision.

I wonder how old I am.
Who ages faster, I or time?

Hundreds of years invade my body,
atomic dust invades my lungs.
How can I be released from the wheel of time?

My age in physical time is certain.
My psychological age, veiled.
The mysterious spiritual time,
an instant, endlessly repeated
awaits discovery.

I catch a glimpse of earth, peaceful,
wild black tulips attempting to grow.

I see perfect stitches binding the earth to darkness,
lasting threads in an open wound,

I see stars imprisoned beneath fractured glass
searching for a breath.

I long to embrace my life, but
I have lost my shoulders.

I long to embrace life in my steps,
but my legs are broken.

I long to embrace life in my thoughts,
but my mind is drowning in the past.

How can I embrace life in my heart,
build a boat there?

My soul is striving for harmony with the universe,
a key waiting patiently for a human hand
to let me pass through the gate of the cosmos.

O if only I could see the world from a lighter space.
The leaves of a fig tree offer to be as wings,
my eternal friend blows breath into them.

My fragile wings flutter.
I start flying.

Fire

Every night the moon dresses in one of her thirty wonders,
each day the sea flows and ebbs with the tide,

every moment I connect with my true self,
in every blink of an eye, my life suspended,
and each sunset I wonder if it's my last.

Then, between earth and sky,
I call to you, my everlasting friend,

and, though you may never hear me,
you lend me your heart, your vision,
your eternal childhood open to miracles.

The warmth of your soul passes through time,
the vibrations of your voice a rhythmic chant;

your palms on my shoulders give me wings,
your friendship travels through all seasons.

You shape language with the mistral,
your heartbeats inviting the stars to dance.

You are here, and there, stronger than time or place.
Far away as the North Star, close as my breath.

Our friend the guitarist on the river's edge
Sings for the river, the water ripples
in tune with him.

I embrace the pearls of the current's flow,
I become, a green leaf, an autumn breeze.

My soul unfolds, embraces
the branches of the world. I gaze
through the trees, my heart opens up
to the breadth of my soul.

Our love travels,
no sound, no land, no motorways,
in complete freedom from space and time.

O love,
I carry you, a foetus in my womb,
the tiniest being with the wildest wings to come.

O love,
stretch your wings, protect me,
let me be the wind beneath your wings.

O life, I merge with you as one,
let me swim in your rapids

O life,
I adore you, don't
drown me.

If only I could stretch out my fingers,
raise my hands, let the stars
filter through,

build pillars of transparent light
for my tent or palace. Light
is the only roof I need.

So don't be frightened, polish
the diamond: the more refined,
the more it shines. At dusk

I collected feathers for you, enough
to grow wings. I picked up

thousands of petals, offered you
the four rooms of my heart,
lit incense at the altar in Jerusalem.

Are you a parrot of paradise
that never returns?
Let us travel in time
to Gilgamesh, believe
in his dream of immortality.

My patience is endless,
my hope remains alive.

How long must I wait:
until the first day of Genesis, or longer?

Come back.

Water

And the rose falls from my hand,
strikes the sea wall, moves
with the Mediterranean waves,
and vanishes. My rose
will never be dry again.

Everything has grains in the heart,
everything germinates.
I found something within
the crown of my fingers,
In the folds of my eyelids.

The roses of the soul flourish in the wilderness,
I dance with flowering fingers,
converse with the moon, it comforts me,
talk to the leaves, they uncover Spring,
whisper to the surf, it carries me.

My soul encompasses new-born stars,
dresses in indigo for the night,

knits the code of the universe,

embroiders its vessel of a thousand petals,

to come back across the Milky Way.

There on the edge of a familiar planet, a shadow

murmurs to me:

Language is an ocean:

words can fill a boat

or overflow it.

The Thames is nearby

the Ganges far away:

let your eyes be the bridge.

The surf is your wedding dress

the waves your bed:

be the pride of the sea.

If a black shadow crosses your room

halt the nightmare:

it's just time to wake up.

When your thoughts dance

without music, create

an orchestra for them.

If troubling thoughts emerge,
touch your forehead:
angels will be their wings.

As the plane's engine rumbles,
it could be the heartbeat
of your guide.

When white clouds pass by
murmur "thank you":
they may have saved your skin.

To know your destination,
let your compass judder:
your heart will be the pilot.

If a mist sits next to you,
let your heart skip a beat:
a rain-cloud will be born.

If you touch your skin
you may feel the whole
cosmos surrounds you.

If you dream of travel,
let a cloud be your boat,
an open space your destination.

Abandon all your houses:
your palm is the vessel
and clouds are your home.

If you search for your lost soul
look into the water. There
dwells transparency of the self.

Don't fear the moment
when death comes like an arrow.

On my way back I rest in the vessel, wondering:
"How light can I be?"

As light as a drop of water
in the river, a sip of wine.

As light as my wings in my mother's womb,
or as a star illuminating a cave.

133

As invisible as the ocean of tears of my life,
or a soul orbiting around my body.

As weightless as streaked lightning,
or as Kew Bridge over the Taj Mahal.

As a breath invisible, visible, or a
seed in the autumn wind.

Air

Which land have my feet just lighted on,
which leaves dance for the wind,
which sky warms the green grass,
which river whispers to lovers passing by,
which world enters my room?

Music echoes over the fields
where my heart leaps,
neighbours protect my dreams,
mimosa teaches me the scent of life,
Buddha caresses my white hair.

Tonight the music is my home;
I may lie down, close my eyes.
Some journeys take a second,
others need more than a lifetime.

Each sunset when the lights of the city
reflect on the river, when the shadows
of trees take refuge in the water:

infinite numbers of suns shine,
their rays warm my heart,
reviving all my senses.

O, I don't lament the sun,
I have many invisible mirrors,
thousands of suns.

Each time when someone deeply, warmly, listens to me,
astonished, I hear my own voice.

My face takes shape
my body feels taller
my feet dance.

I feel lighter and lighter
the sky becomes so blue
the earth seems so tender.

Inner reflections emerge.
I am seeing myself once more.

I have a voice of my own, a face of my own,
a past of my own; I will mould

my own future. I am my life.
I can rise from the ashes.
I will sing.

Ether

When an opera singer's cadence
brings tears to my eyes,
and the cirrus clouds feel

like an oak tree s roots

when the aura of a new day
brightens my eyes with gratitude,
then the disabled child I was

can cross the universe on foot.

I step across the clouds;
my soul carries me on its palm,
returns to the source s arboretum,

becomes one with the universe.

My soul, this is your aria,
oratorio, mother tongue,
a halleluiah raises me to heights

Where all is boundless, free of gravity.

The music wings me to the tropics of the Milky Way.
There, all is being of light.
There, all is wholeness,

there, all is at one.

About the author

Fathieh Saudi was born in Jordan. She completed her medical studies in France and worked as a paediatrician in Jordan and Lebanon, mainly with disadvantaged children. She has been involved for many years with the defence of human rights, peace and justice, particularly in the Middle East.

Over the last ten years, since moving to the UK, Saudi has been particularly interested in writing poetry as a means to express the interweaving between individual and collective issues and how we build our perception of the world around us; how, through our own personal path, we connect with a collective human language that aspires to the furtherance of justice and peace in the world. Saudi has also been concerned with interfaith and dialogue, the meaning of exile, women's creativity, literary translation and language.

Her poetry publications include *Prophetic Children* and *River Daughter*, both in English, and *Bint Al-Naher* in Arabic. She has given poetry readings and performances in the United Kingdom and other countries.

Her previous publications include *l'Oubli rebelle* in French and *Days of amber* in Arabic. She has translated several novels, poetry and scientific books from English and French into Arabic, including *La cause des enfants* by Francoise Dolto and *From A to X* by John Berger.

She is the recipient of several awards for her humanitarian and cultural work, including *Chevalier de l'Ordre du Merite* from France.

Currently she is Board member of English PEN, Committee member of Exiled Writers Ink and member of the Society of Authors.

Acknowledgements

I would like to express my heartfelt gratitude to many of my friends for their comments and advice on this collection. Their guidance, kindness, support and understanding will remain so precious and unforgettable all my life: Anne Rodford, Genie Lee, Jay Ramsay, Mona Saudi, Hana Saudi, Andrew Harvey, VA Harvey, Ursula James, Dia   Batal, Sally Thompson, Graham Fawcett, Tania Naser, Anne Marie Teeowissen, Abdel ghani Abou Alazem, Faisal Darraj and Mahmoud Darwish.